Venice, California

Center Books on the American West

George F. Thompson,
Series Founder and Director

Venice, California:
A Centennial Commemorative in Postcards, 1905-2005

by Delores Hanney

Center for American Places
Santa Fe, New Mexico, and Staunton, Virginia

PUBLISHER'S NOTES: *Venice, California: A Centennial Commemorative in Postcards, 1905-2005*
is the fourth volume in the series *Center Books on the American West*, created and developed by the
Center for American Places. The book was brought to publication in an edition of 3,000 paperback
copies with the generous support of the Friends of the Center for American Places, for which the Publisher
is most grateful. For more information about the Center for American Places and the publication of
Venice, California: A Centennial Commemorative in Postcards, 1905-2005, please see pages 68-70.

The Center for American Places, Inc.
P.O. Box 23225
Santa Fe, New Mexico 87502, U.S.A.
www.americanplaces.org

Distributed by the University of Chicago Press
www.press.uchicago.edu

9 8 7 6 5 4 3 2 1

Library of Congress Cataloging-in-Publication Data is available from the publisher upon request.

ISBN 1-930066-40-6

CONTENTS

PREFACE AND ACKNOWLEDGMENTS

My whole adult life I've been an amateur historian of Southern California as it was during the first half of the twentieth century. A new way to wallow in the ambiance of this place that is my passion opened to me in the 1980s. The revelation came in the form of a book: *Greetings from Southern California – A Look at the Past Through Postcards* by Monica Highland (the name assumed by Carolyn See, John Espey, and Lisa See for their literary collaborations). Paging through the volume and letting myself get lost in the breezy prose and delicious, softly tinted images is still one of my favorite ways to while away a quiet Sunday afternoon. It also inspired me to undertake a postcard collection of my own.

Postcard collecting began modestly enough, but grew to a hobby of epic proportions with the annexation of Ebay as a search tool. To keep it all manageable, it became necessary to approach the quest with a narrow focus. And thus I came to Venice.

Without the desire of my son, Jeffrey Cruz, to help make his mom's dream come true, you would not be holding this little volume in your hands right now. Untold hours were devoted by him assembling and reassembling the elements of this book for presentation and in preparation for printing. My daughter, Samara Jacobs, plunged into the project with equal gusto, remaining gracious throughout changes and edits and re-writes. For their love and support, words of thanks are inadequate but offered here as weak expression of what my heart holds.

Heartfelt thanks go to George F. Thompson, too, for believing in a little book mimicing old albums, and sheperding it into reality.

Venice, California

Greetings from CALIFORNIA

505 -BEACH BETWEEN VENICE AND SUNSET MUNICIPAL PIER
VENICE, CALIFORNIA

California was always a magnet for dreams and schemes—some brilliant, some bizarre. Abbott Kinney imagined an "elevating" cultural renaissance, then developed Venice of America to bring life to his vision. It opened on July 4, 1905

Gondolas on the Lagoon at Venice, Cal.

The Lagoon at Venice, Cal.

Built on marshland, a lagoon and miles of canals were dredged and lined with weeping willow, gum and palm trees. Charming villas were erected for new residents, pretty tents for tourists. Connected to the Pacific Ocean by two large pipes that ran beneath Windward Avenue, the canals were flushed by action of the tides.

Canal, Venice, California.

796 Canal and Tent Houses, Venice, California.

BOATING ON THE CANAL VENICE, CALIF.

U. S. Island and Canals, Venice, California.

Bounded by three of the canals, a
two-acre land mass known as
US Island was the site of thirty-four
one-bedroom bungalows. Operated as
an apartment complex, the units were
rented out furnished and colorfully
landscaped. amenities included a
grocery store as well as commodious
laundry and sewing facilities.

Henry Huntington's Pacific Electric red line provided transportation to Venice from all over Southern California. Local transportation was provided by gondolas, a miniature train, and—until the crowds rendered them a menace—personal vehicles called roller chairs.

2405 – ELECTRIC TRAIN ARRIVING AT VENICE, CALIFORNIA.

Venice Miniature Railway.
Windward Avenue. Venice. California.

Roller Chairs on the Broadwalk,
Venice, California.

Innovative concepts in urban planning included digging several interconnected tunnels under Windward Avenue so that hot salt water could be pumped into hotel rooms for therapeutic baths. The tunnels also eliminated the need for ugly power lines.

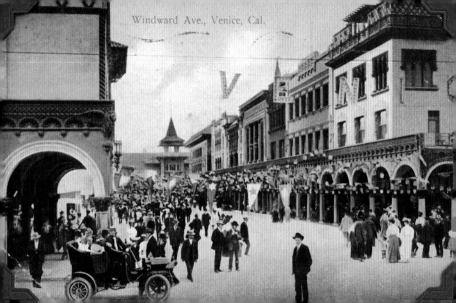
Windward Ave., Venice, Cal.

The Pier at Venice, Cal. at Night

The original 1,700-foot pier was damaged by storms prior to the opening of Venice. Before rebuilding, a protective breakwater of Riverside granite was constructed. The elegant and popular restaurant Cabrillo was built atop the pier. Despite its galleonesque appearance, it was unseaworthy.

View of Venice, California, from Pier.

Interior, Ship Cafe, Venice, Cal.

There were art galleries, dance and concert pavilions, and an auditorium seating 3,600, which was built as a venue for cultured presentations and chautauquas. Alas, public taste proved to be less lofty; thus, Sarah Bernhard in "Camille" gave way to Buffalo Bill and the circus.

Band Stand at Venice, Cal.

DANCE PAVILION, VENICE, CAL.

Auditorium, Venice, Cal.
Ward McFadden, Prop.

$20,000. Aquarium at Venice, Cal.
Free Admission to Balloon Route Excursionists.

The aquarium was a stellar example of abbott Kinney's concept of Venice as a place of elevating entertainments. Designed as a laboratory for studying Pacific marine life, it functioned as both a University of Southern California research station and as a successful tourist attraction.

When the public demonstrated an emphatic lack of enthusiasm for amusements of the highbrow sort, Kinney, as pragmatic as he was idealistic, created the Midway Plaisance by importing all of the exhibits and entertainments that had lined the entrance way to the popular 1904 Saint Louis World's Fair.

798 – ON THE MIDWAY, VENICE, CALIFORNIA.

I am going to take the train back home. M.D.E.

Scene at VENICE, Cal.

The Giant Safety Racing Coaster
"The Race Thru the Clouds"
Venice, California.
Thomas F. Prior, Vice Pres. & Gen. Mgr.

The Race Thru the Clouds displaced
the Midway Plaisance in 1911, to
sprawl like a delicate behemoth
beside the lagoon. Twin cars on 9,000
feet of parallel wooden tracks, ascending
then plunging, rocketing along at
breathtaking pace, exciting, inciting
with madcap thrills.

Crowds gathered like grunion—the silvery little fish that pitch themselves onto California's beaches during certain high tides—to watch aquatic events from the amphitheatre. Auto racing and air shows also attracted thousands of spectators.

THE AMPHITHEATRE VENICE, CAL

TAKING MOVIES OF THE MINIATURE TRAIN. VENICE. CALIF.

The early years of the twentieth century were also the early years of movie making. The process then was spontaneous and resourceful. Plots developed around whatever was going on that particular day; streets became sets. The exotica and bustle of Venice made it an irresistible location to movie makers.

An every day crowd on the Beach, Venice, Calif.

The primal lure of the Pacific required no development. Visitors hunted moonstones and seashells on the shore, picnicked on the sand, flung themselves into the cool, salty waves where playful dolphins were sometimes encountered.

Construction of the Bath House in Venice was a contested project, saved from destruction by a battalion of picnicking women and children aglow with pleasure of purpose. A warm sea without riptides, the heated salt water plunge was the largest on the West Coast.

Surf Bathing at Venice,

New Bath House at Venice, California

Interior of the Bath House, Venice

Windward Avenue, Venice, California.

By the late 1930s, Venice was a dream
in decline. Due in part to sanitation,
in part to politics, and in part to the
new realities wrought by the automobile,
most of the canals were filled in to
become streets, the lagoon to become
a parking lot.

In 1929 oil was discovered in Venice.
The pumping wells completed the town's
transformation into a shabby slum
by the sea. By the 1950s, beatnik artists
and poets were drawn to the cheap
rents in Venice: a rather ironic,
bongo-beating renaissance of culture.

OIL WELLS, VENICE, LOS ANGELES, CALIFORNIA

T403

For decades, the site Kinney had selected to hold his dream of a cultural oasis would languish in splendid seediness, the neglected stepchild of the city of Los Angeles that swallowed it. At last, Venice emerged from its slumber like a butterfly with attitude—a Technicolor manifestation of Abbott Kinney's own artsy vision.

a centennial
Postscript

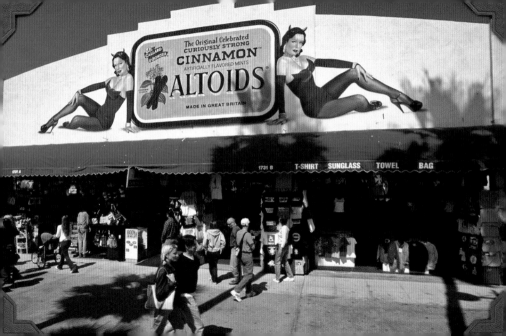

A century later, flocks of daily visitors come to Venice, captivated by the town's funky character, the golden sun, and the ceaseless sea— just as they were in those halcyon days at the beginning. Civic fluffing and puffing, undertaken in the 1990s, served to broaden its appeal without neutering its compelling weirdness.

Though roller chairs have given way to roller blades and skateboards, it is still possible to find resplendent echoes of Abbott Kinney's Venice, such as the lovely villas hugging the banks of the remaining canals, or the colonnaded St. Mark's building on Windward Avenue.

As L.A.'s Left Bank, the area is rife with poets, writers, and artists of every stripe, from film makers to sand sculptors. Gaudy murals are prevalent and such a signature element of the place that the Chamber of Commerce provides directions for a three-mile walking tour that takes in nearly two dozen sites of this public art form.

against a backdrop of kooky shops and tattoo salons, a motley menage of jugglers and dancers, musicians on wheels, fire blowers, weight lifters, surveyors of personal opinion issuing their rants through hand-held boom boxes, and much more offer a banquet of oddball entertainment.

Every day is a carnival in Venice;
the mind boggles to contemplate the
community amped up to celebrate
itself. Given its eccentric style and
quirky cast of characters, the Centennial
will be most memorable. Planned
events are art shows and film fests,
history tours and fireworks, picnics
and parades. Mardi Gras by the beach.

CREDITS

All postcards are from the author's collection.

Image credits for *A Centennial Postscript:*

Boardwalk: Richard Nowitz/Nowitz.com
Skateboarder: Richard Nowitz/Nowitz.com
St. Marks: Pam Gore
Canal: Giampiero Ambrosi/Virtualtourist.com
Mural: R. Cronk
Street Performer: Richard Nowitz/Nowitz.com
Palms: Richard Nowitz/Nowitz.com

By day she brings hope of greater abundance to low-income seniors. By night she travels the streets of Southern California, as they once were, in her mind – reading, writing, remembering, reveling. Delores Hanney grew up in Los Angeles, arriving as a tiny toddler at the end of World War II. Her passion for the place dates to that beginning. Perhaps even before that. Sometimes in dreams she slides across the silken lagoon in a gondola, or sways sinuously on the back of a camel making its way along the midway, or thrills to the whip and whirl of the clackety roller coaster. Venice dreams. Her postcards return her to those early years of the twentieth century.

ABOUT THE CENTER

The Center for American Places is a tax-exempt 501(c)(3) nonprofit organization, founded in 1990, whose educational mission is to enhance the public's understanding of, appreciation for, and affection for the natural and built environment. Underpinning this mission is the belief that books provide an indispensible foundation for comprehending and caring for the places where we live, work, and explore. Books live. Books endure. Books make a difference. Books are gifts to civilization.

With offices in Santa Fe, New Mexico, and Staunton, Virginia, Center editors bring to publication as many as thirty books per year under the Center's own imprint or in association with publishing partners. The Center is also engaged in numerous other programs that emphasize the interpretation of place through art, literature, scholarship, exhibitions, and field research. The Center's Cotton Mather Library in Arthur, Nebraska, its Martha A. Strawn Photographic Library in Davidson, North Carolina, and a ten-acre reserve along the Santa Fe River in Florida are available as retreats upon request. The Center is also affiliated with the Rocky Mountain Land Library in Colorado.

The Center strives every day to make a difference through books, research, and education. For more information, please send inquiries to P.O. Box 23225, Santa Fe, NM 87502, U.S.A., or visit the Center's Website (www.americanplaces.org).

The text for *Venice, California: A Centennial Commemorative in Postcards, 1905-2005* was set in Cochin.
Book cover title was set in Engravers LH Bold Face.
The paper is acid-free Thai A, 157gsm weight. The book was printed and bound in China.

For the Center for American Places:

George F. Thompson, President and Publisher
Amber K. Lautigar, Publishing Liaison and Assistant Editor
Ernest L. Toney, Jr., Chelsea Miller Goin Intern
Purna Makaram, Manuscript Editor
Dan Petroski, of Gecko Imaging, Inc., Image Preparation
Dave Keck, of Global Ink, Inc., Production Coordinator

Special acknowledgment to:

Jeffrey Cruz, Book Designer
Samara Jacobs, Scribe